Mommy Mission:

The complete guide to parenting on purpose

By Keosha L Hinson

This book is dedicated to my children. You inspire and make me want to be my best, even when it seems hard.

To my wife, thank you for always supporting me. You complete me and, without a doubt, make me better.

To my mother, you were right. There is no such thing as the word "can't."

To the parents that have effed up, brush yourself off, forgive yourself, and keep going.

And to everyone with the red squiggly line beneath their name, you were never meant to fit in.
You were born to stand out.

Table of Contents

"God will never give you
more than you can handle,
so clearly he knows that you
are a badass."

Introduction

W hy did you become a parent? Being totally transparent, I did it because I thought it would make him stay. I thought that a baby would make us a family. I did not understand in the slightest bit what being a mother really entailed. What I truly failed to realize, until later on in life, was that I could not control anyone else's behavior... only mine.

I decided to write this book because I was living my life on autopilot and had no idea what my purpose was. I was working a job that I was thankful for, but I was not in love with or fulfilled by it. I realized that I couldn't constantly "preach" to my children about them making an impact in the world and being great if, in fact, I was being mediocre. I realized that I was being a hypocrite to my children.

God has a way of breaking you down and dismantling you just to build you back up and make you better. It took a tragedy for me to realize what I was doing wrong; it took becoming uncomfortable and having long talks with God for me to improve and grow. I know that every parent will not have a tragic life experience like I did and some will realize the damage they have caused when it is too late. Parenting takes a village, so I decided to share my tragedy and errors with the world so that other parents may be able to recognize that they, too, have room for improvement.

Let me forewarn you, growing into the parent that you want to be is going to mean that you must grow into the person that you should be. (That is going to be hard AF.) Before you walk in the shoes of the person that you want to be, you are going to have to step out of the ones you currently wear.

In the pages that follow, you will see being a mother has helped me to grow into the woman that I was always destined to be. My intentions as you turn the pages are that you see that change begins with you and that being a parent is the best thing that you could ever grow through!

"Our blessings are sometimes in disguise, and we just have to be willing and open to let God come in and bless us how he sees fit."

1

God sent me a wife

How did I end up here? The place that I thought was going to be my happily ever after had turned into a nightmare. I was in Atlanta all alone; my support system had somehow faded away. I had two children and was working a job that was barely making ends meet. Nonetheless, I was doing it. I was literally depending on God and had faith that he would work it out. I have found out that it is when you think that you are in charge that God steps in to show you who he really is.

I was lonely, and I was curious. When I was 11, I found a Playboy magazine in a closet that I was not supposed to be in. That became my pastime, in addition to playing with my Barbie dolls. The first time I saw a woman's naked body, it felt like I had fireworks in my pants. I decided to give Internet dating a try. I never really saw what two lesbians looked like, and my mom never really told me that it was wrong. I mean, she was pretty upset when she caught me and my friend playing house on top of each other. She was also upset when she found out my uncle was playing house with me. I just assumed my mom was

1

upset because I was too young to have feelings of fireworks in my pants.

I joined some LGBT social media sites and went on some blind dates, and I was actually kind of discouraged. I had this vision that women had to be better than men because all the lesbians that I knew seemed so happy. But, I was wrong, wrong, wrong. I dated some bad apples. The plus side was that I didn't have to deal with baby mommas. Eventually, I got the "ding" that changed my life forever. We talked and talked. You know, that new-love-talk-all-night-on-the-phone kind of deal. Yup, that was us. I was upfront about what I wanted because I was, and still am, a direct person. We decided to meet at a local club. Immediately when I saw her, I couldn't help but notice the Karl Kani shirt she had on. It was 2010. Nobody still wore Karl Kani apparel. She was nothing like I thought I wanted. I mean, I didn't really know what it was that I wanted, but when I saw her I thought, "She ain't it."

We decided to be friends. What could it hurt? She had just moved to Atlanta from Kansas City, Missouri, and I was in Atlanta all alone. My children were visiting my mom for the summer, so it was really just she and I getting to know each other, without any distractions. We went to eat together and talked about our future and our past. Although I didn't think she was what I wanted, I learned quickly that she was just what I needed. I wasn't really sure what I was supposed to do or who I was supposed to be, so I started off just being myself. Our relationship was amazing. I had a best friend and a lover all in one. But, as the summer came to an end, I knew I had some explaining to do. My son was 10 at the time and already understood what it meant to respect people who were different from him. I had already set that foundation in him. Still, I was nervous. Although, this woman was perfect for me, she had to be perfect for my boys, too. I decided when I became a mom that I would not sugarcoat things for my children. I would always be honest and transparent but still age appropriate. My girlfriend (at the time) and I took my son out to dinner. I explained the dynamics of our relationship and that I loved this woman in a way that I had previously loved men. My older son took a moment to process everything but his response blew me away. At 10 years old, my son looked at me and said, "Well mom, if you chose her, she must be really really special." I cried and felt relieved. That was the first time I was able to sit back and look at my 10 years of hard work. My younger son's reaction was a little bit different, but she grew on him.

Remember I told you I was in Atlanta alone, had two children, and was working a crazy schedule? I had no idea how my boys were going to get to school. I was literally just walking by faith and not by sight. My girlfriend took on that responsibility for me. She took my younger son to school and picked him up. She was my lifesaver. I never knew how God was going to bless me in my time of need. I never thought for one second that he was going to send me an angel in the form of a lesbian lover. Let's face it, so often we hear that being gay is wrong and a sin. I never thought that the God that I served would send me someone in the form of a same-sex partner. The love and support my wife has given me has changed my life for the better. She has, without a doubt, helped me to become a better mother. Sometimes we miss our help, and I think that it is because we think that it is supposed to look a certain way or appear when we want it to. I have learned that God doesn't work like that. He is always on time and always gives us exactly what we need. We sometimes sabotage our own happiness simply wanting it to fit a mold. I think that because I let my guard down and allowed God to come into my life and to bless me how he saw fit, he blessed me with an amazing woman. Now, seven years later he has blessed us, after five unsuccessful attempts, with a beautiful baby boy through intrauterine insemination/artificial insemination. My wife and I always tell the story about how we knew that we were right for each other. My wife says she knew that I was the one when she started singing a church song, and I was able to finish it for her. Our blessings are sometimes in disguise, so we just have to be willing and open to let God come in and bless us how he sees fit.

"He knew that not even YOU could change the plan that he has for you."

2

God makes no mistakes

It was January 21st, and I had received a call from my wife while I was at work. She was frantic because the front door to our home was wide open. January in Buffalo, New York is marked by freezing temperatures and often heavy snow. Naturally, she thought someone was in our home. My wife then proceeded to do a walkthrough of our house with a bat to make sure no one was in there and that all of our belongings were still there. Everything was all clear. Nobody was in the house, but why was the door open? We later found out that my older son had been rushing out the house for school. He thought that he had closed the door when he left, but he had not. Because it was such a cold and windy day, the wind had blown the door open. My son was 14 at the time and, like most teenagers, he was careless with a one-track mind. He was definitely at a stage in his life where we were trying to teach him responsibility. He constantly lost or forgot things, with some of the recent things being his graphing calculators and PS3. This was something else that included so many "what ifs" and could have ended badly. My wife explained to our son how unsafe his actions were and the importance of checking the door to make sure that it is locked in the future. My wife and I decided early on in our relationship that we would not double-team the boys. If one of us disciplined them, the other would not. When I walked in the house from work, I asked both boys how school was and their responses were normal; that was that. It was over…or so I thought.

My wife and I had plans to go bowling, but for some reason we both were feeling so lazy. We sat around dressed and ready to go for at least an hour. All of a sudden, we heard a loud boom. Our dog was going crazy barking and running up and down the stairs. My younger son was paralyzed with fear and screaming that his brother had a knife. I ran upstairs and my wife stayed at the foot of the steps . I saw my son lying on the floor having a seizure and foaming at the mouth. I was terrified. My youngest son was screaming, and so was I. All I could do was hold my son and let him know that I was there with him; he was not alone. As I think back to that time, I wish I had comforted my younger son better. I wish that I had reassured him more. I have forgiven myself for the lack of support that I gave to my son, and I know that he has forgiven me as well. As I held my older son, I screamed to my wife to call 911. I assured my younger son that everything would be ok as I closed his bedroom door.

As we waited for the paramedics, my older son had stopped having a seizure but was still unconscious. Once the paramedics arrived and secured him to the stretcher, he began to regain consciousness. I smiled and told him that I was there. My sweet, loving, patient boy looked like someone I did not know. He became combative, so the paramedics needed the help of the other first responders to restrain him to get him out of the house. As I rode in the front seat of the ambulance, my thoughts were racing. Did my son have epilepsy?

When we arrived at the ER, everything happened so quickly that it was all so surreal. I wanted the doctors to diagnose my son with something that would be easy for me to digest… but somehow I knew that would not be the case. I gently rubbed my son's arm and asked if he had taken something. He could barely speak, but I watched his lips as he whispered "yes." We were making progress. I didn't have any narcotics in my home, so how bad could it be? Maybe some Tylenol or Nyquil here and there. You know, the regular cocktail of items that you would find in a medicine cabinet. Then, I asked him what he took. His response rocked my world. It left me speechless. He told me that he had taken everything. After telling the nurse what my son said, she wanted me to remember every medicine I had in my cabinet. I couldn't recall, so my wife went home to retrieve the empty bottles. The hospital staff requested my son's urine sample. As I assisted him with the sample, he started to have another seizure. I was absolutely terrified. I screamed for help and was asked to step out of the room. I paced the hospital hallway and prayed. I had never prayed so intensely in my life. I asked God to give me one more chance. I promised God that if he gave me more time with my son, I would do right this time.

It seemed like the whole hospital went into the room with my son, but no one came out. I couldn't breathe. I started to think about the type of mother my son thought I was. How did I appear to him? Did I show up in the same way to other people in my life? I prayed again. I pleaded with God for more time with my son. I get it now. I was chosen. God had sent me on an assignment, but I had not been performing up to his expectations. I thanked God for the warning. I prayed that it was a warning. The doctor approached me, so I quickly said "amen." The doctor explained that my son was very sick and weak. Whatever my son had taken was slowly shutting his body down. The doctor said that my son could not continue to fight off the drugs and perform his regular bodily functions, including breathing, on his own. They would have to put him in a drug-induced coma so that his body could recover.

My wife returned with all the empty bottles. Just like I thought, they were the normal medicines that you would find in a medicine cabinet. One bottle stood out. It was hydrochlorothiazide, my high blood pressure medication from the pharmacy. Hydrochlorothiazide is a diuretic used to treat high blood pressure and the accumulation of fluid. It works by blocking salt and fluid reabsorption from the urine in the kidneys and causing increased urine output. I remember I had eight pills left in the bottle, but the bottle was now empty.

My son had been in a coma for six days. As I sat in the family room of the ICU, I couldn't help but think that I had failed. I did my best as a single mother, but I had failed. My child, who

I had invested so much in, didn't want to live. I looked around the room at the other parent whose babies were sick from an unpreventable disease. I felt ashamed because this parent was crying for their children to be healthy and for the doctors to do their magic. I was crying because my son didn't love me enough to say goodbye. I was anxious. I wanted my son to wake up. I needed answers. My wife and I could not understand how our child who showed no signs of depression and had never expressed suicidal thoughts was lying in front of us in a coma from an overdose. Why did he do this? As I look back, I can see how selfish I was about the whole situation. I made it about me and what I was doing. On the seventh day, the doctors had good news. My son's vitals were great and there were no signs of a seizure, so they decided to slowly wake him up. They moved my son out of the ICU and prepared him for discharge.

I couldn't understand why the doctors never discussed his suicide; they never talked about his posttreatment with me. There were no suggestions for psychiatrists or anything. It was almost like they didn't consider what my son had done as a suicide attempt. Honestly, I had no idea if this was normal, so I reminded my son's doctor that my son was a patient because he wanted to die. I literally said those words, and the doctor seemed uncomfortable. Being in the ICU with my son for a week gave me a lot of time to think, pray, and listen to God. I was not going to bury my son; that was not an option. After I inquired with the medical staff as to why a psychiatrist had not been sent in to speak with my son, they sent one in to follow up with him. The psychiatrist spoke with my son for maybe 15 minutes, came out and said, "Your son will be fine going forward. He is sorry that he attempted suicide, and he has hopes and dreams for the future. He does not need to be hospitalized and requires no future care from my team. But if you choose to do so, a counselor may be beneficial." I was speechless. Was this the normal process? Did he really just go down a generic checklist to determine if my son could remain safe? Was this process effective? I was ignorant. I had never had a child who struggled with mental health. I didn't know anyone personally who had a child that struggled either, so I just trusted what the doctor had told me was the truth. What did I know?

My wife and I sat down and had a talk with my son before we left the hospital. We got serious and asked him what happened. My son told me it was his constant screw ups that included him losing his calculator and PS3, and then it was the door. He said the door was his last straw. My son said that it was a combination of things…it wasn't just one thing. He felt that because he continued to screw up that life would be better without him here. I had spent so much time pointing out the things that my son was not doing right that I hadn't invested enough time praising him. I knew without a doubt who I didn't want him to be, so that is what I worked on. In addition to the small events that had taken place, my son said that there was one more thing that contributed to his attempted suicide. He pulled out his phone to play a voicemail. I had been through his phone, read text messages, and browsed his social media messages to try to find a reason why he committed this act. The one place I had not checked was his voicemail. My son played a voice message from his father, who screamed into the phone and told my son he was never going to be anything. My ex told my son that he wasn't proud of him and that he was no longer his son. I remembered the incident from six months prior that led to his father being so upset and leaving this voicemail. My son had been listening to this horrible voicemail every day for the last six months; he had slowly started believing everything his father said. My heart broke for him. My son and his father had always had a strained and unhealthy relationship. His father had his own mental health issues that he left untreated.

I could not begin to understand the effects that that voicemail had had on my son. I gently removed the phone from his hands and deleted the voicemail. I explained to my son that sometimes bad things happen to us so that we will have a testimony and be able to help someone else. I explained to him that it sucked for his father to be the way he is, but God makes no mistakes. I told my son that he was alive because God knew that he was strong enough to handle it. I truly believe that God has already preset the trajectory of our lives. Naturally, we sometimes want to go against the grain. But if we just have faith and trust God, he will never steer us in the wrong direction. God would never want us to harm ourselves to get what he has for us.

"God sends us help. We just have to pay attention and listen for his voice."

3

Recovery/prayer couldn't fix it all

I t was time to go home. No services were put in place. No one provided me with any phone numbers to call. Not one person said a thing about aftercare. At the time, my son had been in eighth grade and had missed about three weeks of school. Friends and teachers had visited him in the hospital. There were rumors circulating about why my son had attempted suicide, so when he returned to school it was very difficult for him. He wasn't the same kid that I knew. He had become hypersensitive and took everything personally.

I got a call from my son's school that he was in the guidance counselor's office distraught and expressing that he wanted to harm himself. The guidance counselor explained to me that they would have to call crisis services. I didn't want crisis services to go to my son's school and embarrass him even more. Honestly, I had no idea what crisis services even did, but I knew that I didn't want them at his school. I chose to take my son home and call crisis services myself.

Prior to this incident, my wife and I had had several discussions about my son's recent behavior. Dealing with children like my son is what she does as a profession, and she is amazing at it. I don't know why I did not trust her judgment. Looking back, I think I was embarrassed and being selfish. I was offended because she said that our son needed help that we could not give to him. When my wife spoke those words, all I heard was that I wasn't enough. The care I provided for my child was inadequate. My marriage became rocky because my wife and I constantly argued about my son's needs. I was his mother. I was the one who prayed that God would help me to give him everything that he needed. Right? Wrong! A light bulb eventually went off in my head. I was able to see how many marriages had ended because of a traumatic event and differences of opinions. I loved my wife, so I had to remember how she had sat in the hospital with me for 10 days. I had to recall how she cried with me for a child that she did not carry in her womb. She had been my help when I wasn't sure how I was going to make things work in my life. I became so mean and nasty to my wife, yet she was so patient with me. She didn't deserve how I treated her. She was his mother, too. What I now understand is that children deserve a village, whatever that may look like. It is necessary to come to the realization that sometimes children are going to need things that parents cannot always provide. The hard part is to find who can.

I called crisis services, and they sent a team out to speak with my son. It seemed like a normal conversation, but once they were finished they told me that my son was a danger to himself. Based on their evaluation, it was determined that he was not able to remain safe. As much as it hurt me, the truth was that my son still had a long way to go. I went with my gut feeling and listened to my wife. I gave crisis services the okay to move on to the next step in their process, which was to call an ambulance to take my son to the county hospital. My son was evaluated again at different times of the day. There were cameras inside of a psychiatric emergency room, and the children's behaviors were closely watched. I needed to get my son in a place where he could be safe and learn coping skills; he needed to be someplace to learn techniques that could help him. Burying my child was not an option.

I'm so thankful for the help that God sent me. More importantly, I'm thankful for my ability to put my pride aside to accept that help. My help came in the form of my wife; I don't know if I would have been strong enough to endure life as a single mother. At first, I didn't think my wife's opinion was worthy because I didn't think she was "qualified." What I didn't know was that God's hand was ALL in our lesbian love, and he prepared her and "qualified" her to be able to walk beside me during this storm. As I continued to open my ears and heart I heard God say, "Faith without works is dead." Prayer cannot fix it all. God sends people in the form of doctors, nurses, wives, husbands, and friends. God sends us help; we just have to pay attention and listen for his voice.

"Owning up to your responsibility is extremely important in any relationship."

4

Own your shit

A
s I signed the necessary paperwork so that my son could be admitted, I thought to myself that I really had no idea what I was doing. After 24 hours of my son being evaluated, the hospital staff had also determined that he could be a potential danger to himself; they suggested that we admit him. I thought that the hospital would be "the magic pill." I thought that my son would be admitted, prescribed medication that would work, learn how to cope with his new feelings and whatever they diagnosed him with, then we would be able to continue to live our "normal" lives. What was "normal" anyway? I didn't know anyone who struggled with mental health, so I was ignorant to the whole process. I didn't have any mommy friends who I could talk to. My son had tons of visitors at the hospital, but it was just my wife and I fighting for him once the dust settled. I did have core family members who checked in on us from time to time, but they did not have any experience dealing with mental health either. They could only be a listening ear. After evaluating my son, it was determined that the help he needed was beyond what they could give him; they suggested an inpatient treatment at the children's

psychiatric center. My son was supposed to be at the county hospital for a couple of days, but his stay exceeded 30 days. He engaged in self-harm with a fork and a screw from the hinges of his bedroom door. My son destroyed the hospital's property and made holes in the walls. The young man that I had raised for 14 years was someone I didn't recognize at all.

While my son was a patient at the hospital, there were countless counseling sessions. It was in one of those sessions that my son admitted to being molested by his stepbrother. I remember when my son was six he told me that his stepbrother, who was nine, had humped him on his butt. I immediately called my son's father so that he could have a conversation with his stepson and girlfriend about appropriate behavior. I also know that typically, if a child engages in that type of behavior with another child, someone has touched them inappropriately. My son's father was so upset; he was at my house with his stepson in less than 30 minutes. The most important part for my son's father was explaining that humping another boy was "gay" and no son of his would be gay. My son's stepbrother was adamant about his innocence; if I were him, I would have lied, too. The conversation did not resolve a thing. I think it scared my son more than anything. Although I told him to always tell me if something like that ever happened again, he never did because he was too afraid. I had no idea that it continued.

As we sat in the counseling session, it broke my heart to hear my son recount some of the abuse that he had experienced at the hands of his father and in his father's care. I did what I thought was best, but it just wasn't enough. I was so focused on creating a relationship with my son and his father because I didn't have one with my own father that I missed how toxic the relationship was for my son.

My son blamed me as well. He said that, although I did not actually take part in the abuse, he felt that I did not protect him. My son could not understand why I felt that his relationship with his dad was so important. He also couldn't understand why I never said anything bad about his father, or why I always made excuses for his dad. It was because I thought that I was doing the right thing. I wanted my son to be able to form his own opinion about his father without my influence. I never thought that so much mental and physical pain would be part of him forming his opinion.

I didn't disagree with my son because his feelings were just that: his. Although my reason for forcing the relationship made perfect sense to me, I had hurt my son. I apologized to my son and asked him to forgive me; that is what he needed to start his healing. So often parents think that apologizing to their children will make their children respect them less. I disagree. Apologizing made my son respect me more. Sometimes a simple apology and request for forgiveness is enough. So many people go their whole lives carrying around pain that an apology or a conversation could heal. After I apologized, everything became so real. I was now part of the problem and that felt uncomfortable to me. Growing is uncomfortable. My son taught me how to apologize even when I felt like my actions were justified. That apology caused a shift in our relationship in a good way; we were able to be honest with each other. I learned how to be accountable.

I think owning up to your responsibility is extremely important in any relationship. I hear so many parents say "do what I say, not as I do." Honestly, who does that help? Parents are their children's first role model and have a duty to show them the way. The role of a parent cannot be done effectively if correct behaviors are not being mirrored for their children. Because parenting does not come with a manual, mistakes will be made often. The key is to own that mistake and be willing to try things another way.

I was so angry when I found out about the abuse that my son had experienced. For a brief moment, I thought of bad things to do to the people that hurt my son without getting caught. I had to stop and think about the only person that I had control over: me. Were there things that I could have done differently? Were there things that I could have done better? Absolutely! I contributed to my son's condition; he had said so himself. I had to stop pointing fingers. Being a parent requires you to "own your shit."

"We don't have the ability to change events in our lives that God has already written just for us."

5

Transparency

After his month-long stay at the county hospital, my son was transferred to the child psychiatric center for additional evaluation. Was my kid really that bad? How many of these other children have gone there, too? Is it like what I saw on television? Where would I tell people that my son was? I had so many questions, doubts, and fears.

After my son's transfer to the new facility, I couldn't help but notice that he was the only African American child. In a sense, my observation made me feel like I was doing the right thing. For some reason, in my community mental health is not taken seriously. The Black community teaches that erratic behavior can be prayed away, or we normalize the erratic behavior and make excuses in some way. I felt as though maybe my son being admitted was too extreme. Maybe all I needed were tools to work with my son at home. Although I had tons of questions, the staff at the psychiatric facility took their time and answered every one of them until I was comfortable and felt safe leaving my child in their care.

My son was angry. He was angry because he was not home. He was angry because he thought everything was his father's fault. I think my son thought that once his dad heard about his suicide attempt he would come around to show his concern, but he didn't. I remember sitting my son down and being completely transparent with him. Sometimes, as hard as it may be, you have to tell your children your story. Let them know who you are and why you do the things that you do. For the first time, I told my son about the abuse I experienced. At three years old, after I was already potty trained, I started wetting the bed. My mother could not understand why. She took me to the doctor, only to find out that I was being molested. When my mother asked me who was doing it, I told her it was a family member. I only had the support of my mother; she was the only person who believed me. Everyone else in my family pointed the blame at my mother's boyfriend, but I knew that it wasn't him. My mother started to take me to work with her instead of allowing me to stay with family. For a long period of time, I don't even remember seeing my family. Eventually I reconnected with my family members, and I was forced to see and sometimes sit in the same room with my abuser. It was family business, so no one really ever talked about it. That was the "normal" response. As I think back, I recognize how incredibly unhealthy and toxic that behavior was to my development.

I told my son my story because I wanted him to understand that sometimes bad things just happen. I wanted my son to understand that the ability to change events in life that God has already written is not his. But his reaction is something that he has total control over. I encouraged my son to smile through it all and make the choice to let his bad experiences be a stepping stone to his best self. Oftentimes parents think that their children will lose respect for them if they really knew the real them, but it is just the opposite. When you are transparent with your children, and anyone else for that matter, they will respect you more. Will there be people who attempt to use your story to try to tear you down? Absolutely. But those people are then displaying behavior that is not even about you

"I was doing all the right things, but I was getting all the wrong results."

6

The diagnosis

W hile a patient at the child psychiatric center, my son was diagnosed with anxiety, depression, PTSD, and psychosis. He was prescribed medication for his psychotic outbreaks, anxiety, and depression, as well as melatonin because his PTSD flashbacks were worse at night. As if that wasn't enough, one of my son's medications caused him to gain more than 50 pounds, which added a new layer of insecurity. While my son was a patient, he was able to visit home. During one of his visits, he was able to graduate with the rest of his 8th grade class.

After my son was discharged, his psychologist was optimistic that he would not return to the center as a patient. In fact, the entire staff, as well as the patients, expressed how much they would miss my son. They spoke so highly of him. They talked about how kind he was to people who were not like him. They were all confident that, because he had a great support system, he would be fine. I was terrified.

My son was referred to a psychologist that the facility thought would be a good fit for him. The site did not even treat children. After a couple of sessions, the psychologists inexperience with my son's type of trauma showed. I hid all medicine and sharp objects. I woke up several times a night to make sure my son was still breathing. I paid closer attention to items to determine if my son could use them as weapons to harm himself. My younger son was happy that his brother was home, but he now felt that he had a duty to make sure his older brother of six years remained safe. I was living a life that I felt unprepared for. I began to do extensive research on what my son needed to heal and became an expert at providing my son with the tools that he needed.

"My change began with me."

7

❖

The beginning of the change

Taking matters into my own hands was the only logical thing that could be done, so I made a plan to be more intentional with my life. Shifting needed to be done on my part so that every word and every action that I executed was done purposefully. Becoming more intentional made it very clear to me that I was not parenting on purpose. If God did not give me more time with my son, the time that we spent together was not very impactful. Sure, I had a good time with my children. We had fun. I loved them, but now I understood that that was not enough. Being a mother was limited to me giving my children what I thought they desired, but their desires were viewed through my lenses.

I remember sitting in the visiting room with my son on one of his visits and chatting with the parent of another patient. This mother had been down this road before. She said, in front of her son, that she always knew he was different because of the Polly Pocket that he begged her for one Christmas. Her son immediately got upset and visibly agitated. He no longer wanted to continue his visit. That mother was not trying to offend her son; she was just recounting a situation the way she remembered it. Based on my observation, I am sure that was not the first time that she told the story; she seemed to not acknowledge how it made her son feel. In that moment, I understood that in order for me to be my best self to my children (and to anyone else in my life) I had to understand what they needed from me. I needed to work on being accountable for all of my actions. When communicating with someone, I needed to ask more questions so that I could fully understand their thought processes. I needed to be more thoughtful about the choices that I made. I didn't want to be perfect, but I wanted to be open to growth.

Perception is everything when trying to build, repair, or nurture a relationship. My son and I were starting over, and I needed to know how he truly saw me. What did he think of me? Perception is reality. You may think that you are doing a great job at work, but your supervisor may see something differently. For 14 years I had been invested in a child that I had given birth to who called me mom, yet I felt like I didn't know him at all. I didn't know if my perception of him was off or maybe I was too focused on other things that I was not fully paying attention. Either way, he and I needed to fix it together. Rebuilding a relationship with my son was something that was important to me; I wanted to be aware of his feelings and how he viewed the world. It was apparent that my growth as a mother would require equally as much growth as a woman; otherwise, my children would view me as a fraud.

For 14 years I had been invested in instilling values into my son that I thought were important, mostly because I wished I had been parented that way. My father is a stranger to me. I often wonder if he thinks of me or even knows that I exist, so it was important to **me** for my children to have a relationship with their dad. There are so many undesirable behaviors that my culture is stigmatized for, but I want my boys to be a part of changing the pattern. My way of thinking limited my parenting to ensuring that my boys spoke well, cared about their appearance, kept their grades above a C, and a whole laundry list of items I constantly found myself correcting. My children meant the world to me. I loved them and wanted them to be great. In their eyes, I wanted them to be perfect. Deciding to parent differently meant learning to understand that I could not change my son; I could not force him to communicate with me. Deciding to parenting differently also meant accepting that all my efforts to keep my son safe by hiding all the sharp objects and locking up all of the medication, could be unsuccessful. All of my efforts could fail! The hopes that I had for my son to respond and communicate with me could only be done by altering who I was. As I began to heal and grow, I saw a shift in my relationship with my children. My change began with **me**.

"As parents, it is important to be mindful and intentional about who we place our children around. Similarly, it is also important to be deliberate about the behaviors and words that are used when communicating."

8

I effed up

After my son's suicide attempt, God really showed me that I needed to pay more attention. There were so many things that my son was doing to cry out for help that I just hadn't noticed before because I was either working or being self-involved. I noticed that my son yearned for attention from girls. He wanted a girlfriend to make him feel adequate. I also noticed that whenever he and his girlfriend broke up or had an argument (let's face it, teenage romances seldom work out), he immediately went into a deep depression. I couldn't understand why my son needed the attention of girls. My wife and I gave him plenty of love and attention. Was he trying to fill a void? Was there something that I was not doing right? Did he require more than I was giving? I assumed for a while that my son was lacking something from me, so I overcompensated. My son's love for girls made **me** feel inadequate and like my love was not enough. One day, I noticed that there was little love left for my second son because the affection, attention, and overcompensation was given to my oldest son. As years went on, my second child grew to understand that most things were the way they were because his brother had attempted suicide.

He felt as though his brother got special privileges and more attention because of it. He was right. I was terrified for years that any small thing that my wife or I did could trigger my older son to make a second suicide attempt. I'm not sure exactly what it was that changed my thought process. I finally understood that parenting my children despite my fears was difficult, but it was something that needed to be done. Parenting is scary because you never really know if you are doing it right. The suicide attempt was used as stepping stone for me to become a better mother and woman.

My son and I had a conversation because I wanted to know why he felt that he needed a female to validate him. Why was it that, at such a young age, he wanted to have a girlfriend/wife, children, and a house with a "white picket fence" without living his life first. I expressed my concern about the way he handled breakups and how fearful I was that one day it would push him over the edge. My wife and I loved him so much, and I was confident that my son knew that because of our actions. During this conversation, I took the time to reiterate the unconditional love that my wife and I had for him. Our love was not enough, and I needed to know why. My son said, "Mom, my need for a girlfriend and the reason I take breakups and rejection so hard has nothing to do with you. You can't fix it. It's in me." He explained that when he was younger, his father's side of the family always teased him by calling him fat or "soft." He told me how bad it hurt that his dad just disappeared from his life. My son said that children in school talked about his darker complexion. He also explained that, although my wife and I always told him he was handsome and that we loved him, he thought that was what we were supposed to say. When a girl showed him attention, it made him feel like all the other bad things he was told weren't true. When they rejected him at school, it reminded him of how his father rejected him. I had assumed I knew the answer to my question, but I was wrong.

Children form their opinions about themselves and the world based on the interactions that they have with adults. Our responses and behavior toward situations have the ability to shape who our children will become. My son was told so often that he was not enough, so that is what he found to be true. I thought my son's behavior was about me. Never considering that his interactions with someone else shaped who he was. The very relationship that I deemed necessary and fought so hard to foster was the very relationship that was toxic and caused my son to carry around insecurities. We, as parents, are in charge of cultivating an environment for our children so that they can grow. Parenting, or lack thereof, plays a major role in the experiences that children have, as well as the type of adults they will become. We have to be intentional about who we place our children around and our behavior and the words we use when speaking to our children. My son's behavior was not about me at all; it was about who he thought he was because of the environment that I had placed him in. I thought that him having a relationship with his father took precedence over how healthy that relationship was. I effed up.

"We, as parents, will not always be involved in every decision that our children make. We must give them the tools so that they are confident to make choices in our absence."

9

◆·❧◆·❋·◆·❧◆

Mistakes are bae

Being a parent, we are expected to nurture, teach, and provide for our children. From the moment they are born, we love them. As they grow, we support them while they learn to walk, crawl, and ride a bike. Although it may be terrifying, we also need to provide our children with the opportunity to grow.

As I began to share my experiences with my son and became more transparent as a mother, I noticed that I was actually fearful of my son making some of the same mistakes that I did. Some of my behaviors may have been viewed as being controlling because I was extremely fearful of my son making his own decisions. I always felt the need to guide his hand. It actually had nothing to do with me wanting to control him; I was just fearful that my son would try to kill himself again if things got too hard. Things had to change. God had saved my son once, so I had no reason to believe that he would not do it again. I needed to become the type of mother that I would be if I was not afraid. . Deciding who she was, that was the hard part. Taking my fears to God through prayer was the only logical thing to do; I needed the strength to trust that he knew what was best. Let's face it, my fear was basically that I didn't trust God. Slowly, I began to tell God that I trusted him every time I became fearful because my son failed. Ultimately, children need to learn how to make mistakes and recover from them.

My older son was like most teenagers; he had no concept of time. In fact, I woke him up most days for school and work just so he could be on time. One morning, he rushed out the house. I thought nothing of it, until I received a call from my son telling me that he had missed the bus and needed a ride. My son decided to sleep in, but I was the one that was going to suffer by being late to work. I was visibly annoyed. It was freezing, and there was about a foot of snow outside. I needed to warm up the car before we took off. My son and I sat in the car in silence as it warmed up, and I thought to myself that I was no longer parenting with fear. As I grabbed my purse with my right hand and opened my car door with my left, I looked at my son and said, "I'm not taking you to work." The look that my son gave me was one with deep confusion. I did give him money to pay for another form of transportation, but I made it clear that the money was a loan. The look of confusion on my son's face was something I had never seen before; it almost made me change my mind. What would I be teaching him if I rescued him after every bad decision he made? That definitely would not go over well in his adult life. I honestly felt terrible that he was going to be late to work and beat myself up the entire morning wondering if he made it to work safely. Later in the day, I received a text message from my son saying "Thanks for letting me fail today."

I smiled. This is what he wanted. He needed to learn from his mistakes; he was just waiting for me to let him.

Providing the opportunity to develop problem solving skills and learning to cope in a loving and supportive environment is the best way to prepare your child for the real world. We, as parents, will not always be involved with every decision that our children make, so we must give them the tools to act wisely.

"As parents, it is important that we do not get so busy that we lose sight of the children we are raising."

10

Everyone has to shine

When I heard the loud boom. My younger son was screaming, "He has a knife!" I didn't know what was happening. I quickly ran up the stairs, not knowing what to expect. My younger son's room was right next to the bathroom. When I reached the top of the steps, I saw my 8 year old paralyzed with fear. Then, I saw my 14 year old lying on the bathroom floor shaking uncontrollably and foaming at the mouth. I am pretty sure that what I saw was on the top of the list for "most terrifying things that a mother could ever see." Choosing which son to comfort first, when they both visibly needed my help, was extremely difficult. As a mother, I think it was natural for me to try and hide how terrified I was by telling my 8 year old not to be afraid and that everything was going to be ok. Closing my son's door to keep him away from the commotion seemed like the logical thing to do, and I never considered how alone or even more terrified that must have made him feel. As I ran into the bathroom, held my older son, and waited for the paramedics to arrive, he was my only concern. My main concern was my older son, who was laying on the floor, because he looked as though he was physically in pain. Ignoring my 8 year old, who appeared to be having an emotional breakdown, was something that I used to think of often. I have had to forgive myself countless times for this. The suicide attempt caused my 8 year old to think that the roles had reversed; he thought he was the "big brother" now. It was apparent that my son thought his 14 year old brother needed to be watched. This was not his obligation; he was only 8 years old. I needed to make sure that he understood that. My goal as a mother has always been to be totally honest and transparent with my children. When I sat my 8 year old down to explained to him what happened with his brother, my goal remained the same. My eyes were red and visibly puffy from crying all night. I knew that my son could hear the fear in my voice. My son seemed anxious and rightfully so because his brother had been taken out of our home on a stretcher. I explained to my younger son that his brother tried to hurt himself so that he could die. I told him that some adults in his brother's life hurt him, so every time his brother thought about that pain it made him really sad.

As I recount the moment when I spoke those words, it was almost like it was still so surreal that I had actually just experienced that situation. My son's face carried so many emotions. If he felt any of the emotions I felt, I bet they included: fear, anger, and sadness. My son stared at me and responded, "I don't want people to hurt my brother. I don't want my brother to die." As parents, I think that it is extremely important to recognize teachable moments when they appear. In that moment I taught my son about suicide and why it could happen. I also took that opportunity to reiterate how important it was for him to tell me if someone touches him inappropriately, no matter what. Furthermore, I explained the importance of communicating his feelings when something is bothering him so that he wouldn't have an emotional or mental breakdown.

My younger son witnessed the progress and regression that my older son made. Although I explained to my son the struggles that his older brother had, he was still 8 years old. All he saw was that his brother was getting all of the attention. My second son started to have issues at school, and I began to receive calls from teachers. The worst part of it all was that both of my sons went to the same school, so my younger son heard all of the whispers about his brother. It was tough for him. He wanted attention, too. Sometimes as parents, we don't take the time to actually try to figure out why our children are misbehaving. We can punish them as much as we want, but there is always a bigger reason. That is where we need to start. I had long talks with my older son mostly because I felt that he constantly needed my guidance and for me to reassure him that he was enough. Well, my younger son wanted that, too. I started to make sure that I was having meaningful conversations with my younger son; I made sure to affirm him daily. Because I knew that my younger son felt that I was showing favoritism, I made sure that I did not discipline him based off of emotion. I always made sure that I had facts to present to him. Oftentimes, I asked him what he thought his punishment should be. Children have a funny way of asking for your attention. They cannot always articulate exactly what they want or need. As parents, it is important that we do not get so busy that we lose sight of the children we are raising.

"God would never want you to harm yourself to receive what he has for you."

11

◆◈◈◈◆

Story interrupted

It was 2:30 AM, and my wife and I were awoken by a loud banging at our door. My wife looked out the window, turned to me, and said it was the police. My intuition told me something was wrong. My heart was racing as I rushed downstairs and saw the police officers flashing their flashlights through my windows. For some reason, I ran past the lights and loud bangs at my door. I rushed into my kitchen, where the lights were on. The sight that I witnessed was so familiar; my son was lying on the floor unresponsive in his own vomit. I was terrified. It was happening **again.**

I got myself together enough to open the door. Someone had called the police. My son's phone was laying beside him and began to ring. It was his girlfriend. I was not fond of her because of the control she had over his emotions. I knew that if he could not effectively manage the feelings he had for her, their relationship would become toxic and detrimental to his mental health. Clearly, I had no idea that it would be this extreme. I answered the phone in hopes that she could give me more information as to why this happened. She explained that she didn't know what happened, but he had taken something. She

49

was the one who called 911. I was grateful to her in that moment; otherwise, I could have woken up to find my son dead. I didn't think that he was in a bad space. I didn't know that he was feeling unsafe. All of the medications were locked up, and I constantly checked in with him regarding his feelings. He had a safety plan. How did this happen? As I knelt down beside my son, I saw the self-inflicted cuts on his wrist. Then, I saw four empty bottles of cleaning solution. Had he ingested them?

As I stood in a familiar hospital, in a familiar hallway for the exact same reason, I could not believe that my son had attempted suicide twice. He had done it again. I was in the middle of writing my book so that I could share my story with the world to change lives and the way that children are parented. Was I doing something wrong? No, it was just the opposite. I was doing something right. The devil had come in and tried to do it again. As I walked down that familiar hallway, I noticed that my prayer was different. Five years ago, I prayed that God would give me more time with my son. I prayed that God would allow me to show him that I was thankful for his blessing that he gave to me in the form of being a mother. I also told God that I would be better. This time, I knew that I had done everything that I could. I had supported, listened to, and loved my son. I gave him the help that he needed and had forgiven myself for all of the mistakes I had made. I knew that I had done everything that God had asked me to do. So, as I walked that hallway praying, my prayer was not for God to give me more time with my son. My prayer was for God to give me the strength to stand tall during this storm. Whatever God's will, I wanted it to be done because I knew that God would never give me more than I could handle. The doctor explained that my son would be fine physically, although he would feel nauseous and weak for a few days..

I was sure that my son's intention was not to kill himself; he was looking for some type of attention. This time, it was not from me. Because of my son's trauma and abandonment issues, he has a hard time handling rejection. Unfortunately, rejection is something he will experience at many different stages in his life. This second attempt allowed me to teach my son about rejection. I explained to my son that rejection is sometimes a blessing; God would never want him to harm himself to receive what he has for him.

God has a way of showing up right when you think that you are in charge. He has a way of showing you that all your trust should be in him. I thought my story was interrupted when, in fact, God was just showing me that my story was not yet complete.

"God will never give you big blessings if you are ungrateful for his small blessing."

12

Role model

My son had either quit or gotten fired from every job that he had, and it was hard for me to comprehend why. My son and I had had several conversations about the importance of working and keeping money in his pocket. He had seen my wife and I work his entire life. Where did he obtain his work ethic from? My son and I sat in the car in a parking lot as he filled out an application for his fifth job. It frustrated me because he had no work history that he could list. He had no former employers that would give him a positive reference. I couldn't help but think that this would be his forever. As extreme as it may sound, I immediately compared my son to all the black men that I know that still live with their mothers as an adult. I compared my son to all of the black men that I know who cannot keep a job, so they turn to illegal activities that will pay them. This was my opportunity to be proactive. I saw a flaw in my child. As his mother, I needed to parent him with the end in mind. As parents, we mostly give orders and assume that we know the reason why. It is extremely important to actually work at trying to understand why our children are acting a specific way; this allows us to parent better. Our children's "why" will not always make sense to us because we have been living life much longer than they have. But at least we can begin to understand their thought processes, which will then allow us to interrupt toxic and destructive patterns before it is too late. As my son and I sat in that parking lot, he was able to share with me something that I already knew. He was able to give me deeper insight. My son wanted to change the world! His young mind did not understand that **everything** we go through, **everything** that we experience, and **everyone** that we meet have purpose. My son didn't think that bagging groceries or ripping off movie ticket stubs would help him to change the world. I quickly reminded him that he does not get to choose what season of his life will get him to what God has for him. The final thought that I left my son with in that parking lot was that he will only gain access to his purpose by being uncomfortable. As parents, we want our children to have everything we have and more. We want them to go to college, get a good job, and live the fairytale life. I want my children to be happy. In fact, I want that to be their number one goal. I have stressed the importance of happiness to my children, as well as taught them that we all are responsible for our own joy. Although my son did not say the words, I knew from his explanation that he wanted to have a job that fulfilled him and had a purpose. Oftentimes people make a ton of mistakes trying to figure out what their "happy" looks like, but I was extremely proud of my son for recognizing that living a fulfilled life was important to him.

This conversation with my son also made me think of some things that I do in my life. I have had many jobs. I get bored quickly. What's wrong with that? Children don't often listen to us; they imitate us. I saw myself in my son. My son had started to imitate the same patterns and behaviors that I had displayed while parenting. Although I was always working, he saw my job changes and witnessed me living an unfulfilled life. He was imitating me. You are your child's first role model. They are always watching.

"I had to heal my trauma and become accountable for my actions so that I would not continue to unintentionally set a negative tone in my home."

13

Contribute vs. contaminate

Being an intentional parent is a role that requires you to be at peace with yourself. You must bring all of your gifts and talents to the table. Your actions have to be consistent, and you must be authentic. Being intentional with your parenting requires you to ask yourself some tough questions; you have to decide what type of parent you want to be to your child. Parenting is just like any relationship; there will be compromises, tears, disappointments, and misplaced expectations. Through all of the ups and downs, as a parent, you have to decide how you show up. Will you contribute or contaminate? Being an intentional parent means that you are constantly contributing to the well-being of your child, being deliberate, and acting consistently. I learned from my mistakes of contaminating. I learned that being constantly critical and feeling the need to always be in control were not always good things. I owned my mistakes and admitted them out loud. I knew that my mistakes were there to help me grow. It was about the recovery and lesson learned. I had other children to raise, so I had to make a plan and stick to it. I had to decide what core values I wanted to instill in my children. The most important part of my plan was the growth that I had to do to become the woman and mother I wanted to be. I had to heal my trauma and become accountable for my actions so that I would not continue to unintentionally set a negative tone in my home.

Conclusion

We think we love someone so much that we want to raise a child with them. We forget to put the condom on or the condom breaks, so we end up raising a person with someone. We fall into the trap of wanting to live by the "social norm" and think that having a baby is next up on our list. There are so many reasons why we become parents, but the most important part of it all is that the child is here. What are we going to do now? What is the plan? As mothers, we often spend so much time being regretful about our role, the way we became mothers, who is not providing us support, and how life just sucks sometimes. Ultimately, regardless of the cards that we have been dealt, we have to seek help when necessary and fill our cup first. We cannot give to a child if we are not pouring into ourselves first.

I overheard the mother of an infant state that she was doing so much better at being a mother than she thought she would. She received a response that said being a mother comes naturally. Immediately I thought of how often a woman who wants to become a mother equates motherhood with being able to wake up in the middle of the night and feed her baby, juggle working and being a mom, being able to have her "me time" and still take care of her baby. How often do people think that's what motherhood is? That's what we see in the media. Women juggling all of these things and still able to remain sane.

As parents, we need to be more transparent. There is no manual, so we are forced to learn from each other and get creative. Children are blessings, but I also think that having a baby when you are not ready to grow or to pour into that child the way that you should does more harm than good to the world and that child. I think that when you are not ready to be a mother and accept change, defeat, guilt, and apologize, you are setting your child up for failure. In essence, when you do that you add another layer of problems to the world because you didn't do your due diligence as a parent. I know my words may seem a little harsh and some people may take offense or disagree with what I say, but I know this to be true because I can honestly say that I was not ready. I eventually grew into the mother that my children needed, but I missed out on times when my boys needed guidance because I was trying to discover who I was. Nobody thinks about hard times because nobody talks about hard times. I know I didn't think that I was going to be a mother who saw her child unconscious at his own hand twice. I didn't think that the things that I was doing would ever affect my children because my intentions were good. Sometimes having good intentions is not enough. We need to be more accountable for our actions, think about the future more often, stay away from making impulsive decisions, write down lists, and plan our lives better. When we don't plan our lives better, we affect other people in the long run. We need to be more intentional, mindful, and begin with the end in mind.

Epilogue

My sons are now 19, 13, and 17 months old. I am extremely grateful for them because I know that, without a doubt, I would not be the woman I am today without God giving me the gift of being their mother. I spent so many years being bitter because I chose the wrong men to father them; that was until I realized that I gained my strength only in their absence. Mothers are tricked into thinking that parenting will always be beautiful, fun, and "as seen on TV." Oftentimes mothers feel inadequate when things don't play out the way we intended them to in our heads. Well, eff the "social norm." Being a mother in today's world takes creativity and not being afraid of not getting it right the first time. The way our grandmothers and mothers parented us would not work in today's world because the world that they raised us in no longer exists. Also, it may not work for the person and parent that you want to be. My goal for this book was to be totally transparent and give hope to parents. If you happen to eff up, just be kind to yourself, ask for forgiveness, and get back up!

Synopsis

Children do not listen to you; they imitate you!

Intentional parenting is about beginning with the end in mind. It is about clearly defining the qualities that you want your child to have and mirroring that behavior through your actions daily for them to see. Let's face it, parenting is never easy. However, the decision to be, or not be, an intentional parent can have long-term consequences for the children, as well as others.

In Mommy Mission, Keosha Hinson will share how her son's suicide attempt caused her to reevaluate her parenting style and admit that she had some growing to do as a parent and a woman. It is hard to admit that one must grow as parents to be better.

In this book you will:

- Learn the importance of being transparent so that your child will respect and know your story;

- Decide the inner values, not the outer performance, that you want your child to possess; and

- Understand why it is important to find ways to respond to your children, not react.

Parents have aspirations for their children, but sometimes those dreams are lost in everyday struggles. Parents sometimes forget that God gave them children as an amazing blessing to change the world.

Keosha is a first-time author who knows firsthand how difficult parenting can be. Keosha realized how she was showing up to the world was affecting how she was showing up as a mother. and she wanted to start over. Keosha became the leader of her transformation and is dedicated to helping other women be the leader of theirs. Keosha is a phenomenal woman who wears many hats and strives to be better today than she was yesterday.

www.ingramcontent.com/pod-product-compliance
Lightning Source LLC
Chambersburg PA
CBHW021200090426
42740CB00008B/1166